Full Moon Midnight

Belinda Subraman

ROADSIDE PRESS

Full Moon Midnight
Copyright © Belinda Subraman, 2024
ISBN: 979-8-8691-2552-1

Cover Art: Belinda Subraman
Editor: Michele McDannold

Roadside Press
Colchester, Illinois

TOC

*Dedicated to my daughters,
Anna and Sunny.*

Writer's Block

Like a frozen hell of winter nights
no home, no blankets, no words.

Gravestones stare from the
amorphous chaos of loss.

A feathered serpent hibernates
refusing to move.

It thinks and dreams
remembering snow

and the welcoming of fire
illuminating shadows.

A loving memory cracks the ice
and warmth blooms from the inside.

Your smile reflects in a window.
Gratitude will save you.

Valentine's Day

Love is a long, bright scarf
in the wind
a hat losing itself to the streets
the inner flap of your loose jacket shining
nature tossing your hair in my face
kissed with a tease of Spring and stamen
buzzed with co-existence with bees.

I salute our flavors
our multi-tongued love
respect for creation
our various hues
of artistic expression.

Love is realizing
it was always a test.
Every second counts.
Everything lasts forever
and everything changes.

A mist lifts
and gifts a rainbow.

Insomnia Again

In these insane times
I tell Alexa to play
rainforest sounds and she does.
The 4k tv plays the war on Ukraine.
A tyrant threatens a nuclear plant
while some politicians
cheer him on.

We're killing what sustains us
with singular egos
and loss of connection
creating dramatic times
living in a pandemic
on the edge of a war
that could wipe the earth
of its human infestation.

Nature will win.
New life will rise
from our ashes.

4:00 a.m.

and no sleep.
I tried forest sounds
including a stream and an owl.
I tried happy tv:
traveling, remodelling
other animals in their habitat.

I tried counting breaths
and soft music.

I tried acupressure
and the mantra
"be here now."

I tried silence
and the static was deafening.

Pills aren't working.

My recurring depression
blossoms in a toxic reality.
I tuned into WW3
thinking avoiding it was not working
and that didn't work either.

Over 3 million refugees
from Ukraine have run for their lives.
My heart races for them
as my body slowly disintegrates
and the world as we know it
explodes and burns.
Annihilation a possibility.

Night is too dark
for sleep.

Anyone Else Awake? 2:00 a.m.

In every war women and children are killed.
Hospitals and schools are bombed

while the opposing side claims it held weapons of war.
Let's pretend war is precision and polite in its killing

and a crime only happens when we notice the truth.
Meanwhile thought manipulation goes unnoticed.

Price gouging is shielded by blaming the President.
Media continues to sell us

whatever they think we might buy with persuasion
while bombs land close to a nuclear plant

and threats of long range missiles are made.
News repeats scenes of destruction

between commercials
of what we don't need now and never did.

I Can't Be Poetic About War.

I can write about the pain, the blood, the killing
the explosions wrecking lives forever
the heart torn screams of mothers
holding dead children
the blood and entrails spilling from bodies
dead or dying
the search for food in bombed fields
and empty stores
the dazed and wounded wandering
homeless.

I can write about
the fear of all things ending
before its time
the horror of invasion
terror without provocation
the proclaiming a reason
while spouting propaganda
shielding hate with greed
the taking of everything a country holds dear
the taking of a country
the lack of compassion
the making of a hell on earth
for the sake of vainglory
bodies be damned.

Spring, 2022

The Pandemic is waning but still present.
Now the threat of WW3 blossoms before Spring.

Evergreen mesquite and cacti
are unchanged
as I learn more friends are dying.

The still bare trees are pregnant.

Weeds are already here
but green and flowering.
I leave them
and love them for now.

Each year Spring is more important
to see the brown and withered wake up
to know everything lives again.

Earth Day

I nurture self-planted Mesquite trees
outside my desert home.
I do not "own" the land
but my husband says he does.
He'll do with it as he likes.
He says he's boss
and he wants the new trees gone.
I'm the one who tends the greenery
mostly cacti, creosote and sage bushes
front yard and back. I water and trim
and painfully "weed".
(I welcome all green
because so little grows here
but I do this for him.)
He declares the Mesquites will disappear.
They're not following the rules.
I plead, "Please don't. I nurture them."
Now he's bought a chainsaw.
I know his plan.
Soon I will be gone all day, selling art.
In a last ditch effort and in vain,
I'll leave a note that says
"Please don't kill what I love."

Greedy Gray

The gray of pregnant clouds
before the water breaks...
Moist air
breathing hard
limping through light.

Weather has its own reasons
though we call it science.
We can predict
but not control it.
It threatens to drown
burn and freeze us
wash the earth's face clean
as slowly we poison ourselves extinct.

Strangers Boarding a Plane

A three year old and I
play a blinking game.
She blinks, I blink.
I blink, she blinks.
She smiles, I smile.
She acknowledges her future.
I acknowledge my past
aware of time
in a blink of an eye.

My Dream Life Saved Me

Anxiety and depression
overdosed my youth.
The unbalanced girl
squeaked by on dreams
and wit.

I attended my father's death
in the same room that was mine
in this house
his own hands built.
I stayed beside him his last three days
with implosive intensity.

I'm visiting that room now
where also I napped, five years old
curled up on a coat in the floor
before a bed was put in.

I am both nailed to and freed by this room
It was death and new life.
I discovered orgasm here.

I have returned to leave again.
Reincarnation.
Yadda, yadda.
Cycle of life.

I am happy now
but know it can change
in the wind
or a dream.

Visiting My Mother

Power is tyranny
in the hands of the hurt.
Pain is transferred
if not healed.

Sounds of comfort
surround me.
The house purrs
through baseboard grates,
the furnace white noise
of my youth.

The brownie page
in the heirloom cookbook
is chocolate stained.

It wasn't all bad.

To Bathe or Not

I honor my father's soap
twelve years since he's used it.
It sits untouched in it's dish
on the lip of a cast iron tub
remembering perhaps
it was the last object
to touch him intimately.

No one cleans here anymore.
Water comes out yellow
with chunks of rust
to remind us
everything decays.

I'm told I may bathe
if I can make the water run clear
and don't use daddy's soap
letting the DNA
of my father linger.

This neglect
is a ritual of love
not cleanliness.
It is a shrine
not a tub.

I pay my respects
by noticing
and find clean water
elsewhere.

Trees From Childhood

I hold on to innocence-
the light
before the darkness
of damage lingers.

I played house with rusty tin can lids
as plates picked from garbage
dumped in the woods.
(It was more the norm than exception
in pre-Earth Day awareness.)

The "standing people" in the forest
were my friends
with arms for swings and climbing,
scent of pine needles and
sticky residue gifted from
the easiest trees to climb.
Delicate golf ball size seeds
were pretend eggs
acorns were pickles
or whatever the menu required that day.

I would serve imaginary people.
It was lonely but they didn't complain.

Why It's Hard to Visit

Maybe it's the years of calling my poems silly
and useless because the lines didn't rhyme
and stealing my outgoing submissions
from inside the mailbox
before I was old enough to drive
or leave home.
It's no wonder I took my poems
when I left in a hurry.
Everything I left behind, mother
threw in the woods to rot.

Or maybe it's because she complains
when I call at the appointed time
that she's eating or brushing her teeth
or her son next door is calling and she's got to go.

Or maybe because, even though she has help
I must wash the sheets, clean my room
and move the junk she's stored there
before I can rest after nine hours
of layovers and connections.

Or maybe it was the nights I sat
with my dying father in the hospital
but when I came home to rest
she made me vacuum, dust
and cook instead of sleep.

I was born in the boonies
where the male elders
were mostly alcoholics
and the women, bitter with religion
raised daughters as domestic slaves
and punching bags for disappointments.

How bad she must have had it
to have been so hard on me
and how unaware I was
raising daughters of my own.
May they forgive me.

Southern Storms

A hurricane is coming in
two thousand miles away
in a land where slaves were legal
and I was raised.
It's a fertile land
damp, thick with mist
and fireflies
a fairyland and asylum
where vines choke flowers.
Your own clothes beat you
in gale force winds
and people are blown away.

Egos mourn, hoard
and count losses...
ghosts afraid of dying.
They are the sting
of your own hair
slapping your cheeks
in a parental storm.

A bitter mother
digs up fifty years
of pain while
black mold eats her closet
with the dankness of a long past rain.

Naming It a Mental Illness Doesn't Make It Easier

I'll never forget the humid darkness
of a summer Carolina storm
in the house my daddy's hands built
sixty three years ago.
Never again. The last time was the last time.
She sold the house.

She made it easier to swim
knowing I was seeing
the Titanic beginning to tilt.
Shame and punishment.
She never took power.
She took revenge.

Her fear transformed to anger.
Always a victim in her solo game.
Always naming violators
of her unknown rules.

One mixed metaphor from a prize.

We're too far out in the water now.
It's cold out here.

There are bees in the clover of mothering

but I'm always thrown back
to the scent of grass
after mowing
releasing essential oils
its rebel yell and kiss
leaving beauty
in the wake of demise

Remembering Last Century

raised on Santa and angels

always a promise of more and better
even after death

met my hero in church
with simplistic 60s guitar
a starched collar version of hip
misguided facsimile with flutes
harmony with hormones
soft voice, sweet face
on the rough edge of dreaming
and unknown projections
karmic ties
chaotic fate
fire

meeting Oz
and a god

searing my spine
with a light touch
of politeness
through a coat, a dress
mythology electrified

ratified with radiating
orgasmic energy
temporarily insane
but satisfied

Depression

A metaphorical sun
is always trying to rise
but doesn't.
Flat blue butterflies
wing gracefully but in circles.
A quarter moon shines brightly
but from the ground.

I try to alter my mood
but I'm stuck with anxious energy.
My kitty keeps checking on me.

I'm old and my friends
and family are dying.
I'm also growing
toward the ground.

I'm wanting to connect
but needing to numb
trying flow therapy
while grasping words.

I am pushing through
aware I'm fighting chemistry.

My kitty keeps checking on me.

Fear at 92

you feel your body breaking
cutting cord
melting chain

aging eyes are search lights
exposing layers
of all intentions

memory fading, morphing
106 degrees
halfway to boiling

hell
is the shadow of no one
creeping in the dark

Mystic Ear

behind the muffled rumble
of central air in an old house
and possible thunder
ruffles of music
moody as weather
cracks a dimension
bifurcates wisdom
in a dance of all creation

but if your god is made of stone
if you wear a symbol
of ancient torture
if you kneel to power
with your pants down
and barter
for existence
clinging to myth
yet let your children disappear

you may never hear
the music of the universe
above the din of humanity
in the free fall of loss
over the tinkling of fairytales

Theocratic Authoritarianism

The ghosts of Southern Baptists
whisper judgements in my ear.
A quick pithy realization comes.
Criminals waving "holy books"
rule the world.
We were raised
to accept the plan,
not see what we're losing
or what we never had,
to blame the wrong people
for the wrong things.

They give us movie myths
where "right" always wins,
where the man is a prince,
the women is protected
and love is everlasting.

But women are struggling
to claim their bodies
as their own
with a threat of prison
if they dare.
They are ordered to bear
future soldiers
but wrap it in religion
and tell us it's what God says.

Anxiety Yoga

society smirks at weakness
mental disorders
no matter what is said about compassion

for some people
panic is a primordial chaotic reality
the Scream as Munch depicted
the dark side of our heart-squeals
where babies are left crying unattended

we all think
no one else suffers like this
where a tight nebulous fear
grabs us by the heart and gut
seizes the brain

some of us become artists
paint with words
humbly stumble over syllables
hoping for writer's zen
where thoughts bloom and clarify
maybe a poem happens
and anxiety does yoga with hormones
in a warrior's pose

if we continue to search
desperately for relief
we may find and practice Pranayama
count our breaths
until shallow prattle fades
along with judgments

where we are cradled eventually
in a womb of quiet joy
birthing oneness
and the struggling afflicted
find peace

July 4th, 2022

Didn't feel like celebrating.
Just another day with a mass shooting.
Shots rained from a rooftop into a parade
celebrating the freedom and ease
of randomly killing, the popular sport
of crazed white boys
unaware they're projecting
killing for power
over something other than themselves
chuffed and gloating
knowing they will be heroes
on the dark web.

Meanwhile, we are "free" to live
with threats of destruction
by white boy tools of the NRA
who can easily buy
weapons of war
but not a beer.

July 4, 2023

Tonight is a time of lighting fuses
celebrating a dream of a myth
we all buy into.
Two mass shootings today
seeming random.
Sport killing a thing now
for maximum attention.
Fireworks and gun shots
mingle interchangeably.

We've gone further into outer space
than into the depths of the ocean.
Struggles and tests
universal to all life forms.
Outer space inner space.
Ego mind slams boundaries
on infinity.

We cannot conceive
our Celestial birth
ever seeking
communication
with the fire of creation.

but we can create little explosions.

To the Mass Shooters

Unfiltered words, unexamined lives.
Propaganda parrots, insane thoughts and projections.
Pain squeezed inward until the pressure explodes.

Judging without empathy, the very thing you need
to soothe the pain, anger in your unloved life
a cold shell unable to open, a small light needing fuel.
You need attention and you'll get it.

You buy the long gun at the shop around the corner
boxes of bullets ready for random retribution.

They will remember you killed their relatives.
You will make an impression at last.
But you will still not be loved.

Super Moon, Midnight, July 13

heavy triteness jolts a rhythm
tightens the rope of time
all life is blended to antiquity
under this harvest moon

a breeze tickles the leaves
rattles things unseen
water fountain bubbles and pours
in my desert garden of lights

solar flames comfort the painful
beauty of impermanence
a row of chimes ring
with amazement

A Personification of Wind

wind
makes sounds of ducks
mating on metal
mouths its own whoosh as well

wind
sounds of bed springs
vigorously in use
clangs a flagpole,
bounces a canopy

wind
embraces our being
gets intimate with hair
easy to feel souls blowing kisses

Hail to the Jim Webb Telescope

Midnight, July 14

I watched the earth birth the moon
proving we are orbs in motion.
I watched the moon
travel the sky.

I saw the first photos
of space deeper than dream.
I felt tiny in one solar system
among many in one galaxy
among billions of galaxies.

We are creatures on a rock
spinning.
We have learned
we know nothing.

Moon Game, July 15

The wind sailed the moon tonight.
Chimes played in the darkness.
The city light crown
over the mountain fooled me
but no orb reflection formed.
Where did it go?

One by one my loved ones are leaving
to the ether of vastness
where the moon disappears
from mere specks of animation
to blending with everything
where "understanding" is not an issue.

Cycling

stardust dancing
in sun rays-
micro souls streaming
coating elements reshaped
by human hands-
a spotlight glimpse
of star filled air-
a cycle poem of creation
change and connection
that becomes the ground
we walk on
dig in
holder of bones we danced in
under the moonlight

Earth Report

heat advisory
fire danger
air quality alert
a new strain of virus
killing the innocent
monkey pox striking
the intimate
WW3 in progress

politicians trading liberty
and empathy for riches
as houseless numbers grow
weapons of war killing civilians
anyone can buy
out of the trunk of a car
gun show or store
as if killing was encouraged

mass shootings everyday
for sport or fame
our pettiness and politics
and hormones

unknowing in our infinite smallness
that we're toys in the brain of the cosmos

indifferent to the egos
that keep us alive
and disillusioned

we send out signals for connection
fortifying wisdom
we refuse to heed

The Fall

It's the romance of crisp air,
the deep earth scent of brown leaves,
the tickle of oncoming holidays
or the fire of memories
at the hearth of history.

Daylight dampens the slanted light.
A match starts the wood-burning stove,
a fireplace in the kitchen,
a piece of a captured sun
roasting what it grew
with help of human hands.

It's cooperation
in the cycle
in the autumn of human Being,
in the slow decay of age
dragging time.

There's only so far you can go
with topical hip pain relief
and intimacy with a heating pad
grappling with the fact
every version of you is intact
but the inner self is in need
of a new encasement.

You fight it
like the dogs from hell are hungry.
You live with the light of an untamed sun
see every mountain as a mother
from womb water born,
every pool of water sacred.
Time is a river that has no end.
You swim through, are baptized.
You fight it until it swallows you.

Waywardly Mobile

Life funnels breath.
Electric current amplifies.
Humans pray nearby
with tribal understanding
woven into a light seal.

Cathedral windows
power star worship
whittles heaven to fear
curled toward comfort.

Every head is a planet
across time zones and years
transporting to
surrealistic planes,
lives woven into media,
burning injustice,
stinging politics,
shaming preachers
witnessing
a cult of damnation...
seeking bullets instead of love.

Boomers

Eternal youth lingers
in half-remembered fog
with angelic auras
of virgins in the mist.
Ethereal bodies
lightly clinging
to their hosts,
add dimension to being.
It has reached the time
of whatever is, is.
Boomers in mid-century lawn chairs
pull up their lap blankets
and try to remember names.
Their cd players play
"Let it Be."

Reviewing Music That Saved Me

It's a magic cord, a silver bell singing
word storm swirling
chemistry and imagination
caught in a net self-cast
frayed strand of twine
tentacle from the ether
tingling through the atmosphere.

It makes the notes square out
become Egyptian flutes
carved in stone
beguiling mystery and strength
through the ages.

It treats discordant camels
in radiating sand
(an albuterol kind of day)
no water or shade
fever and congestion
cacophony of discomfort
trances me into calm
a universal sigh
of healing.

The Eagles and Everything

1.

Everything teaches us
the circle of our lives
the way the earth spins
the face of the clock
the time of day then night then day.
Inside the circle we intersect
form designs that disappear
ethereal mandalas
somewhat skewed in the atmosphere
glowing mysteriously over mountains.

2.

The sound of water soothes us:
echos of the Womb
sounds of fluid shifting in a personal sea
a heartbeat and oneness
and warmth
then we are born
crying.

The ancient ones soothe us.
We all long for the mothership
and connection

but we can't reach back
the circle goes around
in one direction
repeating itself
a carousal of figures
rising and falling.

3.

Everything in space revolves.
Bits break off and burn
self destruct into another thing.

Failing the lesson of no escape
despite what one believes
nature, the cosmos, every atom and cell
teaches "deal now or later."
All transforms but never leaves.

Today's Attempt

A scarf hides a biopsy bruise
on the throat while I smile
as if my dreams came true
and choking was not an issue.

Walking is painful
but I must keep moving.
I don't want to lose fitness
and my bones turn to dust
before the grave.

Patches, salves and pills
take the edge off
after yoga fails.

Creating sometimes helps.
Paint on my fingers
reminds me I'm trying

and these aching words.

Earth's Green Gifts

It's a substance to peel you from the mirror
a sweeter brand of misery
higher world otherness
froth of creation
where a glide on ice freedom
outweighs the sliding into a wall vision.

It's a parachute for thought
a party in your head
celebrating neurons and synapses
in a mystical meat suit.

It's your chosen sublimation
a mythical halo from fairytales
a floating tattoo of meaning
labeling you as irregular.

It's Peter Pan in the clouds
and Jack and his stalk
adjusting your attitude.
It's you, grateful for Earth's green gifts.

Too Perfect

I awake.
I am in gratitude
for everything, everyone
this moment of typing fingers
and thought.
A tender green awakens.
All beings rise lightly.
Warmth washes all pores.
The breeze kisses.
Patio chimes
clang, tinkle, rattle and drum,
blending with cooing, chirping, hooting
in surround sound.
Cat Stevens'
"Morning Has Broken"
begins to plays on Soundscape radio.

Quantum Friends

Awakened by wind,
thirsty and mystified
by the worm holes of truth.
If atoms are probability patterns
affected by relationships
then truly we infuse
objects with meaning.
A keepsake is a bridge
to the inner and outer worlds.
The sensations we feel
sitting next to a friend
or stranger
is the reading of energy
through shared atmosphere
and atoms.
Our friends through cables
and computer screens
are as real as light
and sound waves
we alter through thought.

From the ancient Indian metaphor
Indra's net:
Pull one thread
and all else is effected.
No act or thought
is secret.
It ripples through the web.

Spirit Wind

Everything is
alive with moving atoms,
all of nature in a subatomic hum.
The wind is spirit
balancing atmosphere
from angry squalls to flirting
in cahoots with the moon.

The wind has many voices
and knows more than we do,
hints at layers of illusions to work through.

Hang the best chimes you can
and listen to what the wind says.

Sunrise, Sunset

Counting life by decades
on fingers
using a second hand
remembering youth
and the other worldliness of age.

The past has not passed
as it's one long day
with gradations
of all we've ever been
caught between the womb and stars
hungering for the hug
of recognition
and dissolving into the void.

Fading Into Morning

taught by a fixed star
and spinning earth
all is a cycle in flux

lung roots inside us
like branches of trees
nature and stars
a forever mystery

like fingerprints in water
our breath caught in the wind
our likeness drawn
in the sand by the sea

is how it will always be

Time Shifts

Feeling auras dim,
pivot, pull away,
cool air rushes in
turning cold,
tearing the membrane
in a couples' cocoon.

Internal hum heightens
and follows orders
from an unknown source
hearing gears

in organic machines
making body waves,
teaching a lesson
in relationship...

emptying and dawning,
healing psychic wounds

until we blend with
spiced forest soil
hot with tiny life.

Disorderly Speaking

I cling to
illusions of comfort
from voices
channelled through cable
on pet TV
controlled remotely

the sting
of beloved dead ones
breathing anachronistically
our friends who never knew us
soul pinched
by attachment

distraction from pain
triggers for the senses
connective
electricity
from the universe

learning and leaning in
then freeze-stroke panic
role switching white noise
shielding knowledge
of the war within

neurons burst
submissively
inhaling through the veil

I may never know
what this is
but I bow
and keep the door open

On My Birthday

It's a night where all is miraculous.
Soundscape channel plays
space music with nature pics.

Uplifting quotes flash by
invoking gratitude
for all that's gone.

A tv nightlight
sparks positivity
life captured in frames.

Feline feet warm against me
akashic memory streams
through a body in decline.

I feel a web of yin yang
in the womb of the world
with three remotes.

Straining through fog
anything but stopping
in awe to have lived this long.

Birthday at Ojo Caliente

Snow still on the ground-
air below freezing-
greenery yellowed to hibernation-
"Only Whispers Allowed"
written on a lit paddle
carried by the watcher
and knower of all things
reminds us to check
our propensity for touching
in the sacred milieu
among ancient stones.

Scantily clad we enter
caressed by the hot eye waters
connected to the boiling core
miles beneath us
and the limitless sky above.
You put your hand on my knee
saying "Be my anchor"
and we are
for each other.
You the floater
me the rock
this time.

Dying, #12

the romance of the unusual
the glimpse over the horizon
the depth of a waking dream
on a higher ethereal plane

in a body breaking down
adapting to deficiencies
leaning in to find
a conduit of connection
the focus grows
toward a gentle end
a fading
a joining
a whisper of smoke
rising
a sudden knowing
a belonging

The End

morning rainbows last longer
in slanting Fall light
the twilight is hope
in all directions
and sensual dimensions
your companion in bed
is machinery and love
awash in white noise
tidal breath bi-pap and
oxygen concentrator
the heart swells as birds
suddenly rise together
flutter specifically beyond the sky
you go joyfully
fading into the sun
burning into light
whether or not
you ever yawned an Om
or mumbled a Baptist hymn
now you realize
everything

The Moon After Christmas

Mind trap hangover.
I retain a plastic angel
battery powered
with a humming glitter swirl
- humankind transformed
cosmic energy-
manmade aurora borealis.

It's color-changing water belly
on a revolving crystal stand
transports to another realm

touching invisible shields
between mini-motor noise
and the slow croaks of frogs.

I'm winding down now.
Like the plastic angel's energy source
I will transform again.

I will be the moon's reflection
in water
waving and dancing in the wind.

Inventory Without Punctuation

the background hums of comfort
gentle breath of air conditioning
the slight click in the fan on low
hanging from an angled ceiling

the occasional shift of a paw
of a cat under cover or its soft snore
it seems the bed is sleeping

trying to feel the atoms
and auras outside myself
looking back through a now lens

the infrequent sounds of a car
in a cul de sac street
desert cacti with arms outstretched

the love of two cats and a mate
lost and floating
all with brain cells shrinking

the painful response
to creaking walls
felt in my hips on a heating pad

my computer phone
and Amazon Alexa
all listening

no protection in rejection
we are monitored everywhere
even our thoughts

finally seeing
as my eyes grow dimmer

broken lazy scared words
find a brave mouth with spices
swat cliches in a buzzing mind

the sharp claws
of a loving cat
tries to milk me

symbolically
suddenly jumps down
love confusion over

remembering it is a cat
who likes to sleep alone

Zen

death is lights out
like a coma or surgery
but we won't wake up
the self imposed suffering
of not mattering enough
to live forever
in movies, books or legend
any lasting alter of love
degrades our lives with pangs

we are comforted knowing
our dead loved ones
will reach for us as we die
hallucination or hope
we like it

we choose to believe
in magic and forever
to smooth the jagged edge
and illusion of finality
one of many realities
we fail to discern
as every molecule
around us prickles
beams life force

sparks
and radars connection

we clutch
still we fade away

into the cycle
of mattering

where everything is enough

Coping with Grief

Grief is a burden
I clutch
the way I pull my coat tight
in cold winter winds
when sleep is on the edge,
a promise of relief coming
but never arrives.

I play this game where
being claustrophobic
and introverted
sets up a special tension
as if a character
in a video game
is controlled by virtual lever
in another galaxy then
drops through a black hole
where all is reversed.
Mirrors there are cyclic fluidity.
Memory becomes DNA
and the psyche is set free
floating beyond time
where dreams are reality
in a swelling silence
and peace is a leaf on a river

A Wink and a Prayer

may we be
infused
with light

light-hearted
light-headed
surrounded by halo

may the peace of being
still us
as we breathe
with the universe

may the night veil
through which dreams shimmer
always have points of light
and clouds glow
even hushed by a new moon

may we crack open ego
and attachment
awake with an orange stretch

may love and morning be married
may morning be eternal spring

Flying In a Dream

Every sense prickles
from tapping of rain on the skylight,
purr of the overhead fan,
to the head noise of a thousand years...

A live wire from God
buzzes the spine, buttocks and thighs...
life's combustion and transcendence.

Before fogging into books, letters, sound files
syllables birthing poems
bloom from hypnotic OM

as micro-specks in the fabric of space
electrons of eternity spark
in the cosmic brain...

smoke veils chameleons
and morphs rainbows
in a desert of wings.

Soft Reality

Through wavering auras
invisible antennae
we read and are read
subconsciously

like Saguaro cacti
with the moon in its arms
and the sacred scent
of campfire wood
wafting
through the sky's embrace

The Unattainable Other:
a remembrance

the lights will flicker
the paper turn yellow
the story will morph and disappear

but I hold these moments of
times in India on the backroads
by the Ganges
in the Temples
with my in-laws
protected in a bubble
aura-egg of love

the exotic smell of diesel
a wood fire
incense and curry
flower leis and jasmine strands
dung and dirt

being a foreigner and family
among the sing-song codes of people
with humbly bobbing heads

where every bend in the road
held fruit stands covered in flies
and skinny cows scouring for food

where washing was done by hand
from castes lower than Brahman
and sweeping done by woman squatting
with handmade brooms of straw

where the refrigerator
was in the living room
due to space
but also pride

where oil lamps burned
in a niche beside
statuettes of favorite gods
Saraswati, Lakshmi and Ganesh
knowledge, fortune and good luck

that last visit to Madras
before Chennai and divorce
was acknowledgement of melding
then turning away
a swirl of honor
amazement
family like Norman Rockwell
meets Bollywood on Mars

we were children
dreaming

who grasped and grabbed
while sinking
then went wildly different ways

Homage to Dali

our remains nourish the earth
and all that grows

we're all part vegetable
as well as flesh

thought cauliflowers
sprout into space
as the brain shrinks

the big picture is a feast
with unlimited choices

time is butter

Homage to Van Gogh

I break the seal
on an artist's canvas.
A child sings in the background.
The neighbor's dog watches
as my cat slinks by.

Slowly shrinking to infinity
eye beams connect to everything
music tingles the feet
rain falls from the stars
auras expand to fill
the heart of the universe.
I paint.

What a Picture is Worth

I want to write
create an atmosphere
but the alphabet fails me.
I approach color instead.
My hand moves over a substrate
holding a brush, a cotton swab
a steal ball on a stick
or nothing at all
just hands manipulating color
like a child before it's criticized
back to "normal."
I am happy in this play
and continue until satisfied
then I share with you
my excitement with color
my poetic depiction
my one thousand words.

Throat Chakra Blocked

My psychic DNA
vibraties a mandala
where time bleeds into wind
sun eats clouds
blurs into heavy rains
shouts and Oms
into hums and buzzes
of a rotating world.

Nature ruffles chimes
to a healing chakra song.
Metal sings
vibrations to the bone.
Orange moves over
the face of water.

I fall into a sunset world
at the crack of dawn
where the end is
the beginning again.
Color is my song.

The Answer

I see it now in everything I do~
a hazy hint of enlightenment~
in my handwriting, my painting~
the fizzy vibrations~
atoms dancing infinitely
in the all encompassing unnameable bliss.

It took decades to get here
and it's only in glimpses
when the slow computer of the cosmos
reveals a synthesis instead of an answer
where there is none.

What Remains

I am processing today.
I feel Higgs Boson particles moving,
atoms and planes changing,
loss as tangible removal.
Another death
associated with my youth,
my innocent love
of magic and kindness,
the absence of someone unknown
in person but known
through the media,
their gifts shared globally,
impacting my perspectives,
igniting my cognition
and sharing metaphysically.
We were never going to meet.
We never needed to
but there was comfort
knowing they breathed
created and loved.
Appreciation, admiration remains.
All that I interpreted and received remains

and the bewildering finality of it all
remains.

Science Explained to Trumpsters

Science is the earth dying,
acid rain, carcinogenic crops,
draught, money driven ruin,
galaxies beyond galaxies
black holes of power
and mystery.

It's history
like nesting dolls,
reveals stages of being,
our doing, undoing,
and poisoning
the depths of life.
It's not a trend that is in
or going through a phase
or way to slow business
for billionaires.

It does not disappear
when you disbelieve.
More real than religion,
science is like God unfolding
an ultimate, ethereal essence
that puts man-written holiness
in a shallow fairytale grave
where men walk with dinosaurs
and eat fruit that shames.

Release

It's why the elderly in nursing homes
(the final segregation)
long for their beds
to be left alone
to fill an emptiness
with a jigsaw of dreams
and floating memories
as an untrimmed tree
taps the roof in the wind
as if knocking on the door
to other realms.

They search for
relief from forced feedings
of crushed pills in applesauce
the drawing of blood for lab tests
and glucose monitoring
from sitting in a wheelchair
with a wet burning bottom
watching others
in the same shape in the day room
where the only "activity"
is inertia while
watching weather
through a window.

Death becomes the prize
the knife edge of life
the last hump on the winding road
the shedding of a meat suit
the longed for lightness of being
the solving of a mystery
the build up of dwindling
to the point of no return
...release...
when they can join the wind.

Wordsworth in the Desert, Aging

I need more than knowledge
of nebulous cosmic connection.
I need words and sky maps
connecting dots on the ceiling

in the shade of a mind-forest
drawing life inward
casting visions as sparkling truth
fluid in the human context of time.

My fear: An avalanche of words
dwindles into alphabet soup
word salad on the edge
of a hungry abyss.

I grip near the word summit
of a mountain disappearing
while the lines from the climbers behind
dissipate down the slopes.

A strong breeze blows its notes
syllables disperse randomly
are read by stinging skin
and gritty empathy.

Rain sprinkles on hard packed sand
drops of joy falling like letters
wetness trying to soften
and nourish our desert floor.

Infinite Mollusk

a chambered nautilus
breathing water
exhibits mastery of life
tentacles sensing
fingers in the waves
pointing nowhere

everywhere

the inclusive mind
is love in action

the mind creates the abyss
the heart crosses it

a chambered nautilus
breathing water
exhibits mastery of life
tentacles sensing
fingers in the waves
pointing nowhere

everywhere...

Joy to the World

Joy rises in a new soft bed.
Crickets and flutes
sing of the night.

Thought is plasma
through kinship
common grounds
freedom to Love.

There is something Holy
about this Land.
You cannot drown
in the Dead Sea
cradled in the salty
womb water
of Mother Cosmic Orb
moving through Eternity.

Eternity

Life and Death
dichotomy
yin-yang
front and back
roots and branches
segments
webbing through eternity
above and below
dark and light
multi-cultures
multi-tongues
multi-orgasms
no single thing is true
everything is

A few of the poems included in this collection were previously published in the following publications. Roadside Press wishes to acknowledge them for their fine work and dedication to the small press.

Setu, Lothlorien Poetry Journal, Cajun Mutt Press, *Unlikely Stories, Chrysalis, New Generation Beats 2022 Anthology, Chiron Review, and Impspired, Poetry Bay and Al-Khemia* which nominated "4:00 A.M." for a Pushcart Prize.

Belinda Subraman did not go to kindergarten and did not know her ABCs when she started school. Compounded with dyslexia and punishment for being left-handed she had a hard time learning to read and write. Eventually though, writing became her best friend and still is today. Her first publication was in college and that gave her the encouragement to keep writing and submitting to various publications listed in the *Writer's Digest*. One of her more notable early publications was a two page spread in *Youth Times of India*, edited by Kamala Das. Since then she's been published in hundreds of zines both in print and online.

While living close to Nuremberg, Germany she developed many international literary and musical connections and one day decided to start a magazine. Other editors were generous sending her literary contacts. Bukowski was in the first three issues and an interview with Burroughs was in the second issue of *Gypsy Literary Magazine* (1984-1994). During the same time period she edited books by Vergin' Press, among them: *Henry Miller and My Big Sur Days* by Judson Crews. She also published *Sanctuary Tape Series* (1983-90) which was a mastered compilation of audio poetry and original music from around the world. Beginning in the 2000s she had a podcast interview show that was broadcast on three internet stations in two countries. Through all these venues she's published and interviewed many notable poets, artists and musicians.

In 2020 Belinda began an online show called GAS: Poetry, Art and Music which features interviews, readings, performances and art show in a video format available free on Belinda Subraman's YouTube channel. She also runs a GAS Facebook group and GAS literary journal.

Belinda is also a mixed media artist. Her art has been featured in *Beyond Words, Epoch, Flora Fiction, Unlikely Stories, Eclectica, North of Oxford, Raw Art Review, El Paso News, Litterateur RW, Setu,*

Texlandia, The Bayou Review, Red Fez, Chrysalis, Maintenant 16 and many others. In November 2022 she won 2nd Place in the Sun Bowl Exhibit, the longest running art show in the Southwest (since 1949). Belinda was named Beat Poet Laureate of Texas (2023-2025) by the National Beat Poet Foundation, Inc.

MORE ROADSIDE PRESS TITLES:

By Plane, Train or Coincidence
Michele McDannold

Prying
Jack Micheline, Charles Bukowski and Catfish McDaris

Wolf Whistles Behind the Dumpster
Dan Provost

*Busking Blues: Recollections of a Chicago Street
Musician and Squatter*
Westley Heine

Unknowable Things
Kerry Trautman

How to Play House
Heather Dorn

Kiss the Heathens
Ryan Quinn Flanagan

St. James Infirmary
Steven Meloan

Street Corner Spirits
Westley Heine

A Room Above a Convenience Store
William Taylor Jr.

Resurrection Song
George Wallace

Nothing and Too Much to Talk About
Nancy Patrice Davenport

MORE ROADSIDE PRESS TITLES:

Bar Guide for the Seriously Deranged
Alan Catlin

Born on Good Friday
Nathan Graziano

Under Normal Conditions
Karl Koweski

The Dead and the Desperate
Dan Denton

Clown Gravy
Misti Rainwater-Lites

Walking Away
Michael D. Grover

All in a Pretty Little Row
Dan Provost

These Are the People in Your Neighbourhood
Jordan Trethewey

Radio Water
Francine Witte

They Said I Wasn't College Material
Scot Young

And Blackberries Grew Wild
Susan Mickelberry

Licorice Heart
Miles Budimir

Disposable Darlings
Todd Cirillo